MW00627654

Praise for Wise
Up! At Work

"Everything that Cristina brings into this is very beneficial in terms of being able to stop and look at how I'm approaching work. She's introduced me to a lot of ageless wisdom, and bringing that into the day to day really changes things and my experience with work. I'm really grateful to her for revealing this. I'm just excited to see where all of this is going to go from here." **- Steve Smith, Partner and Chief Marketing Officer, The Starr Conspiracy**

"Cristina's insights into how teams work and how managers can engage their teams effectively are very powerful. Her work is based on timeless philosophy and the human experience. This isn't an app, but rather, real, time-tested strategies that help teams work better together. I love the engagement and the performance that her work delivers." **- Jeff Loehr, Chief Marketing Officer, Red Sapiens**

"All these ideas are relevant to everyday working life, and I think we need to be reminded of some of these things because maybe we don't think about them often enough. Cristina has helped us with a way to be reminded of them. I found the conversations with Cristina around philosophies very insightful." **- Michael Zingsheim, Project Manager and Employee Engagement Specialist for the State of Michigan**

"Cristina provides a new perspective in a way to bring wisdom back to the forefront and think about it differently in a way we may not have thought about it before. The four steps in her framework are very, very efficient. It's very effective. It allows us to be better coaches and managers of people. From all that perspective, it's been very helpful for me. I really appreciate it." - **CJ Warstler, Founder, DecisionPoint Selling**

"Cristina has created a brilliant framework for effecting and executing organizational change. Her work integrates ancient philosophical wisdom with modern organizational theory. She is a pioneer!" **- Gina Lepore, Founder MACH4 Enterprises**

"Cristina's unique approach enhances how the individual functions both in life and in business. I am able to examine potential opportunities better, take note, and observe things objectively, and then to apply these tools provided daily. As a result, I am getting more business, with more experiences and opportunities presenting themselves. I believe this is all because Cristina helped me work on the way I view things and clear my tainted lenses to see things as they are." **- Jennifer Netrosio, Founder of Limitless Lawyers**

"Cristina has a unique command of personal psychology, wisdom traditions, and organizational savvy, which she applies through finely tuned coaching and consulting. Cristina's intuitive questions and sharp perception helped unearth an aspect of my work life that has been a major struggle for me; this was the first time I'd been able to talk about this with someone who could help. Also, did I mention she's fun? Great humor, enthusiasm, and emotional IQ. Highly recommended."— **Rick Sanford, Organization Development Consultant**

"Cristina's compassion, optimism, and practical advice were always a breath of fresh air and truly made an impact when navigating mental roadblocks and outlining the desired path forward." — **Brianna Sykes, Senior Project Manager, Modicum**

Manage with Calm, Navigate Obstacles, Lead the Way

Cristina DiGiacomo

Wise Up! At Work

For information address Goodrich Publishing, 2425 W
Bronco Butte Trail, Unit 2020, Phoenix, AZ 85085

This book may be purchased for educational, business, or
sales promotional use. For information, please email
cristina@moralchemy.com

Published by Goodrich Publishing
Phoenix, Arizona
GoodrichPublishing.com

ISBN-13: 978-1-7339963-2-7

Library of Congress Control Number: 2020936053

Table of Contents

Introduction 3

The Biggest Crisis Facing the World of Work 3

Facing the Crisis 'Head On' 9

Philosophy is Great When You're Staring Down the Barrel of a Boardroom 20

Back to the Future 22

Not Just for Nerds 30

I Kant Do It! 37

This Is the Air Above the Tip of the Iceberg 47

The Corporate Holy Grail 50

Yes, Wisdom Can be Practical. Here's How. 55

Charting Our Course 60

Clarity: Know Before You No 61

The Reality Check 63

What Do You Desire Most? 65

Speaking the Truth 69

Truth Takeaways 75

Make No Mistake 75

I "Need It Now" Version 78

The Grains of Truth 79

On Thinking: The Good, The Bad, The Ugly 83

Don't Go to Last Week's Meeting 85

If You're Happy and You Know it, Overthink 88

You Are Not A Pen 91

Hold That Thought 93

Fighting the Trojan Thoughts 101

It's the Thought That Counts 103

I "Need It Now" Version 106

On Second Thought 107

Decisions: A State of Independence 111

Mind of Your Own 117

Making Decisions is Easier than You Think 118

Getting Good at Good Decisions 125

Decisions, Decisions! 127

I "Need It Now" Version 130

Deliberate About Deliberation 131

Action: When the Stop Gets Going 133

All Booked Up with Nowhere to Go 134

To Act or Not to Act, that is the Question 139

Non-Action and Action and How They Serve Each Other 142

True Action in Action 146

How to Act with Tact 149

I "Need It Now" Version 152

Caught in the Act! 153

Final Thoughts 155

Acknowledgements 159

About Cristina DiGiacomo 161

Hello!

I'm happy you're here.

If you're a corporate leader - CEO, executive, HR, or a manager - and you are facing a major crisis, huge swaths of your business are being disrupted, or more simply your office is a revolving door of gripes, or you're refereeing the same interdepartmental conflict, or that person is still getting under your skin, or you've been up all night worrying ...

Welcome, you're absolutely in the right place.

I have some comforting news. I'm going to introduce you to a few "old friends" who can help.

However, instead of offering you the same, jargonized, business as usual solutions you've heard before - the time management, goal setting, growth mindset, leadership development, resilience, adaptability or "insert latest management buzzword here"- I'm opening the door for you to a whole new reality.

You're about to discover a new approach to the obstacles you face at work. This book gives you simple, time-tested ways you can experience clarity, reduce overwhelm, feel in control, expedite decisions, and be effective.

In short, I'm offering you a wiser way to work.

So what do Steve Jobs, George Soros, Peter Thiel, Angela Davis, Stewart Butterfield, and Alex Trebek have in common?

What do you think Philip K. Dick, iconic science fiction writer, and Carly Fiorina, former CEO of Hewlett Packard, could talk about?

Keep reading, and you'll discover the answer.

Dedicated to all who toil.

"I can, therefore I am."

— Simone Weil, French Philosopher

Foreword

In this day and age, business brings a lot of intangibles – what value do I bring to my clients? How can I innovate an old industry? How do I rebrand myself? Do I rebrand myself? These are questions, among many others, that rear their heads every so often so we must stop to evaluate (or re-evaluate) in order to forge ahead.

Add to that the stress of making payroll, increasing sales, dealing with stressed out employees, and every other possible obstacle put in our way by the daily grind. How we manage it all can be overwhelming, but as leaders, we need to be wise enough and adapt.

I've always said, I want to work smarter, not harder. It doesn't mean you don't work hard. Hard work never killed anyone, but if we're busy tripping over ourselves, or others, to accomplish things, what's the point? It's time to stop reinventing the wheel and go back to basics.

With business running at breakneck speed, it's very easy to get caught in the weeds in order to try to meet everyone's demands and deadlines. However, sometimes we have to stop, think, employ a little wisdom, and remember to breathe. Simple enough, right? Then, why is it so hard to do this sometimes?

Because we fell out of practice.

Cristina's book provides a series of simple and effective ways to help us focus on what needs to be done, ignore the distractions, reduce the feelings of being overwhelmed, and find our focus amidst the chaos. It's a book that reminds us to go back to the basics...but with a twist. Forget the overused buzzwords, and instead, let's put in a little brain power on how we conduct ourselves and how we lead our businesses through the ups and downs.

So, wise up, and read this book!

It's what great leaders do.

Jeffrey Hayzlett -- *Primetime TV & Podcast Host, Speaker, Author and Part-Time Cowboy*

Introduction

The Biggest Crisis Facing the World of Work

"I feel out of sync." My client, a CMO of a consulting firm, was suffering. His work focused mainly on helping entrepreneurs and startups, but whenever he held a meeting, consulted with his client, or worked with his peers, he felt he wasn't gaining any traction.

"I don't understand what value I bring to my clients or if it's even what people want," he told me. "I'm frustrated, and I don't know where to take my work. I feel a lot of pressure to do something, to make something, *anything,* happen, but if nothing's working, I mean, what's the point of all this?"

I knew he was in trouble because he couldn't even put his finger on what, specifically, was the problem. But the underlying issue, the one that kept surfacing as the waves of anguish and doubt kept pommeling him was ...

What's the point?

That's where we started, in the pit of professional despair. We'll get back to him. But he's not the only one suffering.

What I have experienced firsthand, and what I have come to realize, after 20 years of working as a rank and file employee, then as an expert manager, then as a successful workforce leader, and finally as a category creator, is that, at some point, most people get hit with the underpinnings of corporate distress.

I see this over and over in the clients I work with - they aren't prepared for change, they start dropping like flies, get disillusioned with work, leave before their potential is reached, and struggle to make sense of it all.

**What I've found
is most of those
symptoms stem
from what
philosophers
would call an
"existential
crisis."**

The biggest crisis - and the biggest opportunity - facing people in the world of work today is an existential one. It's not just threats from downsizing, bad coworkers who undermine them, or straight-out mismanagement.

The biggest challenge comes from within. This crisis arises, essentially, from the questions people ask themselves or the things they say to themselves about work in their quietest and sometimes darkest moments.

Things no HR department, boss, or board knows they say, and the thoughts sometimes go like this:

"What am I doing?"

"I'm so overwhelmed."

"This is out of control."

"When do I get to work on what I want?"

"That co-worker's a @#$%^."

"Are they trying to push me out?"

"I'm so frustrated."

"I feel a 'vibe'."

"Who am I to do this?"

"Are they going to like it?"

"Are they going to like me?"

"What the heck just happened?"

"I have no time for anything."

"They're faster and smarter than me."

Sound familiar?

Consider that not only you may be asking yourself these questions or telling yourself these things, but also that your employees and your colleagues are holding the very same conversations in their minds as well.

Now, consider the effects all these thoughts have on the capacity they have to do their work to the best of their ability.

How much time do you think you spend on these kinds of thoughts? I once calculated this with a client, asking them to note anytime they had the above thoughts, and for the ones they were actually aware of, they determined that they spent at least two hours per day having these kinds of thoughts.

That's 10 hours per week or **40 hours per month** in which their mind is badgering them.

I believe this estimate is much greater than that for a lot of people - at one point I tested myself, and I found myself thinking such thoughts as many as three hours a day (I was pretty stressed out at the time).

Not only are you dealing with your own thoughts, but also, how much time do you think you spend dealing with everyone else's existential thoughts? In emails, on social media, and in text messages? You're exposed to their random, fleeting thoughts and ideas, and the thing is you're *expected, or conditioned, to respond to them.*

Think about how much time you've spent in your thoughts about their thoughts!

How can anyone get any work done, let alone overcome challenges?

Facing the Crisis 'Head On'

What happens when those thoughts roam freely? Let's say you have an employee who thinks people are out to get them, or they're hoarding information and being territorial, or they've checked out completely. Perhaps you've noticed decisions that are too short-sighted, or ideas and initiatives that are just a bandaid, or people are **burying the bodies of previous mistakes**. Any perspective they have flies out the window, chased behind any and all rationale and reasoning.

Delusion reigns, and chaos is created.

It seems like not one day, or headline, goes by where there isn't a CEO or organization not acting wisely - either greed, or avarice, or envy. You know you've had watercooler conversations about these companies and these individuals.

We could all use a little wisdom. Because wisdom can ameliorate these situations or provide a path to prevent these situations.

What you're going to learn is **acting wisely in the 21st Century is no different than acting wisely in the 5th**

Century. The golden rule, serving the common good, everything is connected, learning from mistakes, not taking more than is necessary, being humane, and so much more.

I've seen shining examples of leaders and organizations who faced this "existential crisis" by acting wisely, especially in tumultuous times.

For example, Intel's new CEO, Robert Swan, recently decided the company's culture needed a shake up, and he instituted measures that fostered unity. The previous leadership believed "Only the Paranoid Survive." Swan instituted a new internal organizational motto of "One Intel". He believes in confronting issues more openly ("honor truth and transparency"), increasing collaboration.

These ideas are rooted in philosophies around collectivism and connection and surfacing the truth.

Here are a few other examples:

- Danny Meyer, CEO of Union Hospitality Group, stopped taking his CEO salary so that his workers could get paid during the Coronavirus epidemic.

- Helge Lund, Statoil ASA's CEO, became a daily fixture in the lives of his employees as an advocate for safety and security after a terrorist attack killed his workers and provoked him to outrage.

- Doug Parker, CEO of American Airlines, instead of fear-mongering about the "sky falling" set up a task force working in close contact with the TSA, CDC, WHO, Health Department to make sure that his staff and customers were safe during the Coronavirus epidemic.

- The CEO's of numerous grocery chains instituted "senior shopping" hours to protect the most vulnerable during the Coronavirus epidemic.

Those are just a fraction of the very public and extreme situational examples of wisdom-driven work and leadership, but there are infinite examples of everyday moments and heroes.

Yet, the tragedy remains that many organizations aren't just not acting wisely, they're going against the very tenets that make the world work, that help us function.

Because of this flagrant fouling of principles, reckonings, and very public reckonings at that, have become quite common.

Transparency is the new black. You no longer can "get away with it" - leadership and companies are being checked.

Perhaps wisdom is the bulwark?

Susan Fowler, the Uber whistleblower, seemed to think so.

"While I was still working at Uber, facing constant mistreatment, I'd made a habit of reading a famous passage by Marcus Aurelius on the way to the North Berkeley BART station each day, to prepare myself for what I'd encounter at the office: 'Say to yourself first thing in the morning: Today I shall meet people who are meddling, ungrateful, aggressive, treacherous, malicious, unsocial. All this has afflicted them though their ignorance of true good and true evil. But I have seen the nature of good is what is right, and the nature of evil what is wrong.' Now, sitting in front of my laptop, I remembered these words ... and those of other philosophers - Aristotle, Plato, Epictetus, Seneca, Immanuel Kant - searching for insight into how to do the right thing and, most important, how to know what was right." — Susan Fowler

If we're all dealing with the latest crisis, running from meeting to meeting, hustling up new opportunities, and monitoring 30 projects at once; if we're all deciding who gets the raise and who gets the bad news, getting one-upped by that partner department, and trying to decide the right next move while simultaneously grappling with "what's the point?" questions, then what are we to do?

What's the solution to these very real and very problematic situations?

The solution, I've discovered, is cultivating wisdom for the working world through Philosophy, or, in particular, a vein of philosophy that I've coined, **Industrial Philosophy**.

What's the First Thing You Think of? Thinking Cap or Yoga Pants?

When you hear the words - philosophy, wisdom, or being a wise person - what images are conjured up? A dude on a mountain with a beard, where people are trekking and dying just to get to see him? Or a guru in yoga pants chanting? Or someone in a room with dusty books, a tweed suit, bowtie, and bi-focals lecturing a bored class of undergrads?

Philosophy and wisdom often get lumped into categories of being too "stuffy" or too "woo-woo," or too "out there."

I'm here to dispel these notions and present you with a different point of view. It comes from what you might barely remember from high school or college as philosophers, the relevant ones, the real ones, the ones whose teachings have changed the world.

The ones who rolled up their sleeves and got to work, dug deep, spoke up, despite hardship, resistance, and even the threat of death. And after studying them...

Here's my definition of Philosophy and Wisdom:

Philosophy is a protocol for engaging with the world.

Wisdom is an active expression and outcome of philosophy.

I'm going to give you five examples (out of hundreds) to show you what I mean:

- Observation and analysis, the genesis of scientific and analytic thinking originated from Thales and Aristotle, and Descartes was responsible for the Scientific Revolution. Many philosophers were the first scientists and mathematicians to discover and set the foundation of the world we live in today.

- Our democratic ideals, the foundations of our government, **the U.S. Constitution, came straight from Plato.** This eventually freed slaves and gave women the right to vote.

- Social justice, human rights, and feminist ideals were championed by Michel Foucault.

- **The wellness movement** - meditation, self-awareness, balance - came from Lao Tzu, and John Locke gave us the method of introspection as a way to better understand ourselves.

- Norms we value in society - **politeness, non-judgment, goodwill,** 'We are all one' - came from Indian traditions and texts like the Bhagavad Gita.

Even the handshake, the way we greet each other at work and close deals, that originated in Greece during 5th Century BC, as a sign of peace showing neither person was holding a weapon.

Philosophy is very much alive and a part of our every day; we just don't know it.

Every revolutionary, human enlightening juncture, science, art form, and all of the best moments of our humanity is all based on philosophy.

Imagine your workforce or your leadership or your organization tapping into the very ideas that moved societies, that inspired people, and that, yes, changed the world. Perhaps I'm getting too lofty, and **all you care about right now is facing that dreaded 9 am Wednesday meeting, constant interruptions, a touch of procrastination, and difficult people who seem to block and tackle all your ideas.**

Guess what?

The sages gave us assistance for that, too.

Philosophy is one of the most important things that can come into the corporate world today because of its fundamental properties and practical benefits. I'm presenting philosophical ideas as the core for transforming the working world.

The good news is you don't have to live like Socrates (with him being sentenced to death and all) in order to be wise. I know how excited you were to grow that beard or learn how to tie on a toga.

All you need is your mind and your ability to question. That's it.

Philosophy is predicated on principles, and we know principles can be the foundation for progress. If progress in a company is desirable, then philosophy makes good business sense.

I believe philosophy meets the needs and delivers the answers for work on organizational, team, and individual levels.

Can You Name 20 Famous People Who Studied Philosophy?

Remember those famous people I mentioned at the beginning of this book? The answer to what they had in common is they all studied philosophy. And they're not the only ones.

Here are a few more:

Aung San Suu Kyi, *Nobel Peace Prize*

Ethan Coen, *Oscar-Winning Director*

Steve Martin, *comedian*

Bruce Lee, *master martial artist*

Phil Jackson, *championship-winning NBA basketball coach*

Gene Siskel, *film critic*

Susan Sontag, *American writer and political activist*

David Foster Wallace, *American writer*

Ricky Gervais, *comedian*

Mary Higgins Clark, *mystery writer*

Gerald Levin, *CEO, Time-Warner, Inc.*

Jimmy Kimmel, *late-night talk show host and comedian*

Harrison Ford, *actor*

Mark Hulbert, *financial columnist for Forbes magazine*

Chris Hardwick, *TV host*

Dennis Miller, *comedian*

Lana Del Rey, *singer and songwriter*

Sam Harris, *neuroscientist and author*

Peter Lynch, *headed Fidelity's Magellan fund*

Patrick M. Byrne, *CEO of Overstock.com*

Robert McNamara, *former Secretary of Defense*

David Souter, *Supreme Court Justice*

Ahmet Ertegun, *founder, Atlantic Records*

Marko Ahtisaari, *Senior Vice-President of Design, Nokia*

Rick Rubin, *record producer, Columbia Records*

Stephen Breyer, *US Supreme Court Justice*

Richard Riordan, *former Mayor of Los Angeles*

Terrence Malick, *filmmaker, The Tree of Life*

Mark Boal, *screenwriter, Zero-Dark Thirty*

Anthony J. Leggett, *Nobel Prize in Physics, 2003*

Nic Pizzolatto, *creator and writer of the television show "True Detective"*

Do you think these people are too woo-woo, stuffy, or out there? Perhaps their success *is* tied to studying philosophy?

Philosophy is Great When You're Staring Down the Barrel of a Boardroom

Many companies are seeking answers, and those answers can come in many wonderful forms.

However, many times, the "solutions" companies come upon only skim the surface of the actual issue, and **over time get translated and reconstituted and forgotten.** How many binders about assessments and change initiatives that haven't stuck are gathering dust on your shelf?

Now, there's nothing wrong with any of these change practices. In and of themselves, these change practices all constitute very good things. But very often, they get watered down when it comes to their actual implementation. And sometimes they're so watered down and so re-interpreted that they don't represent the wise traditions on which they're based.

Yet the core problem remains the same.

"All business problems are people problems." -
David Cancel, CEO of Drift.

So most problems have to do with people, therefore
solving those problems and success in an organization
has to do with people.

If we want to succeed and develop great workplaces,
and we know the crux of it all sits at the human level,
doesn't it make sense to understand and work from
that which makes us human?

Back to the Future

This is why cultures have a hard time changing.

We're focused on fixing the wrong problems - using restructuring, layoffs, and posters in the cafeteria. Recently, I sat down to read a case study about a technology company's culture-building initiative. The headline caught my eye, and I just dove in. Several pages later, as I was reading about how the executives were turning the company around, and I was nodding my head in agreement with everything this company was doing, the date of the case study popped out on the page.

1987.

The same methods, the same ideas, the same problems, the very same management practices we are still talking about, were espoused in this article as a new, right way of doing things. My jaw dropped because this article could have just as easily been written today. It was like back to the future.

My point is this: the answers have been in front of us the whole time. We've just been too busy chasing that shiny thing, or we believe the solution has to be this super complicated, difficult endeavor or else it doesn't justify the effort and its half a million-dollar consulting tab.

We've spent so much time reinventing the wheel it feels we're not getting any closer to the root of the problem to deliver a sustainable difference.

Perhaps we need to get back to the basics and get to work!

Do You Like Oranges or Orange Soda?

You have an orange and orange soda. Neither is wrong or bad, and they each serve certain tastes and certain situations very well. However, applying wisdom at work is like picking a ripe, juicy orange right off of a tree. **It's taking the original idea and using it.** There's nothing wrong with an orange soda that quenches your thirst. But it's not an orange.

By going directly to the source, aka wise thinkers, you hold in your hands the original intentions, the common sense ideas themselves, and **you can then make of them what you will**, as they pertain to your life.

You are the ultimate authority of how something works or doesn't work in your own life. And you can see it for yourself - not experience the reflection of someone else's interpretation.

You hold the orange in your hand instead of someone else's orange soda.

I want to present you with an orange so that you have direct access to the wisdom itself.

The reason why industrial philosophy or real-life philosophy is so important is that it actually helps you do the things you need to accomplish most in the corporate environment - elevate your perspective, do the right thing, and act accordingly.

In addition, most of the important and progressive management, communication, and organizational practices are actually based on principles that are firmly rooted in philosophy.

Here are some examples of what I mean **by philosophy used in the workplace:**

- **"Servant Leadership"** - Helping others and doing your work dutifully come from philosophies of service from the Romans like Seneca and Marcus Aurelius.

- The ideas of **employee-centric cultures and employee-driven suggestions** are a modern expression of the Democratic ideas espoused by Plato.

- **Reciprocity and meritocracy,** mutually beneficial acts (aka, business partnerships), and equitable work cultures (aka, "Everyone is treated fairly") can be traced back to ideas from the Chinese philosopher Confucius.

- **Resilience and "having a voice"** can be tied to the teachings of Ralph Waldo Emerson.

- **Collaboration and Agile** are both expressions of the concept of non-duality which can be found in multiple traditions - Hinduism, Buddhism, Advaita Vedanta, and Neo-Platonic thought.

🖉 **Work/Life Balance** is an outcome that can be traced back to Lao Tzu's teachings on balance in life.

🖉 How many times have you used or heard the sentence **"for the time being"** in a meeting? Do you know that expression and the concept of *time being* is first found in a Buddhist philosopher's poem from the year 1027?

And don't forget that the **handshake** I mentioned earlier, the way we greet each other at work, remains a classic.

What I've found, though, is that people gravitate toward and better process the original ideas from philosophers and then connect and embody those ideas better than the reconstituted names we've given them. You can see this for yourself later in the book.

If philosophy inspired ideas that really changed things, **how many more ideas are waiting to be discovered by revisiting it and its practices?**

All Good Intentions

A common workplace change practice is assessing EQ, aka Emotional Intelligence.

I believe that…

Emotional Intelligence is just another way of saying Wisdom.

Hear me out. Let's take a look at the main aspects of EQ according to Daniel Goleman, the American psychologist who popularized the idea of Emotional Intelligence in 1995.

- Self-awareness.
- Self-regulation.
- Motivation.
- Empathy.
- Social skills.

I'm sure you've all encountered a wise person in your life. People who are wise have all of those characteristics. The only difference between EQ and philosophy is that EQ doesn't quote Socrates directly.

All the practices I provide in this book will help you develop all of these good things.

Furthermore, according to many wise traditions, we all possess wisdom inside.

Therefore, I believe we all have EQ.

You'll see what Aristotle has to say about this soon enough. Just know you are not deficient in EQ or Wisdom (more on this later); it's just your level of *awareness of it* is what varies.

The Difference Between Mindfulness and Philosophy

While I'm at it, I need to explain the **difference between Philosophy and Mindfulness.** Now, you might be wondering (I'm guessing because people ask me this all the time): what's the difference between mindfulness and philosophy? Mindfulness is a practice; it's a practice of a state of being. Philosophy gives us the guidelines and reasoning that encompass hundreds of principles and even more practices.

Imagine a galaxy.

Mindfulness is a shining star in that galaxy.

Philosophy is *the* galaxy.

In my own working life, I often integrate mindfulness practices with philosophy to effect change. When I was instituting a big change at a company I was working for, my guiding principles and inspiration for change came directly from Plato's Allegory of the Cave (aka, showing people how to see the light), but mindfulness was a tool I used to center myself and prepare for engaging with leadership before I led people out of the cave. Mindfulness was the glue that kept all my beliefs, thoughts, and actions tied to the presence of reality as I instituted these changes.

If you are personally practicing mindfulness or working on it, learning more about philosophy will only enhance your practice.

I want to give you direct access to the sources that all of these workplace practices and ideas are based on.

Perhaps you may think that all of this is self-evident, the Captain Obvious kind of stuff. And, yes, it is. But, let me ask you: has anyone taught you **how to execute on that self-evident stuff in a way that it becomes second nature?**

I'm going to teach you the "self" and the "evident" part, no filter or middleman required.

You already have these inclinations inside of you, all I'm doing is helping you draw them out and make them a practical part of your every day.

Practicing philosophy and accessing your inner wisdom is easier than you think.

There's no new language or jargon or framework to understand. And you don't have to buy a new set of yoga pants.

As I said before: Philosophy meets the needs and delivers the answers for work on organizational, team, and individual levels.

It's the right tool when you're staring down the barrel of a boardroom.

Not Just for Nerds

My experience of philosophy and how I explain it to people is it is a *protocol for engaging with the world.* The dictionary says it's discovering the essential nature of knowledge, existence, and reality. This is kicking it up a notch for the working world ...

Here is how I define **Industrial Philosophy:**

The application of philosophical principles and practices for the benefit of the individual at work and an organization as a whole. To discover the fundamental nature of knowledge, reality, and existence within the workplace to foster a sustainable, contented, and productive environment.

Industrial Philosophy is a protocol for engaging with work.

How you see situations, the thoughts you have about those situations, the way you choose to apply those thoughts, and how having those thoughts applied inform your actions and determines how you feel about work.

Your capacity to seek the knowledge, know your reality, and understand your existence at work is the foundation of Wise Up! At Work.

It gets even more interesting when you think about a team's view, thoughts, decisions, and actions represent how they feel about work, and it becomes even more interesting when you consider an organization's view, thoughts, decisions, and actions affect how it "feels" about its work.

It sounds pretty straightforward, and you're probably like "I know all that."

But there's something you may not know:

The Missing Link: Being Wise is Innate; Acting Wise is a Skill.

Aristotle's foundational idea of being human is that we are all wise, inherently. What I'm saying, however, is that the act of bringing forth wisdom in the real world, when the world is uncomfortable and messy, is a skill. Acting wise requires awareness and practice, and I'm going to teach you how to do just that.

That's what you're missing: you know about wisdom, but it's not a skill yet.

So you may *know it*, but are you really *doing it*?

Here's why acting wise is important:

- Google's study Project Oxygen determined that soft skills were the most important skills to work at Google.

- Harvard, Boston University, and the University of Michigan did a study on soft skills training and determined there was a 256% ROI in the areas on retention and productivity.

- A CareerBuilder study cited that 77% of employers believe that soft skills are more important than hard skills.

I say that...

Wisdom is the ultimate soft skill.

Someone who is wise holds a high EQ or emotional intelligence. They can be described as sharp, resilient, collaborative, decisive, creative, adaptable, transparent, visionary, empathetic, even punctual.

All the things you want to be and want others to be at work **ladder up to being wise**. But a person possessing those attributes also needs wisdom in order to apply these qualities in the right measure for the right situation.

I imagine wisdom combined with risk-taking as a potent combination.

So, let's go to the source of wisdom, and everything that's important for success will cascade out of that.

A Word to the Wise

Here's what happens when you apply wisdom for the workplace:

- Less time (and money) spent on multiple trainings for each niche, soft skill.

- A faster rate of change as people get out of their own heads and get on with it.

- More agile environments as people are able to come together, focus, and deliver.

- Higher retention rate, or the right people staying, as they are able to engage with their work and align with a vision more clearly.

We're in a "knowledge economy" now, so it makes sense to examine and exercise how to attain and elevate our knowledge of ourselves and the work we're doing.

For the purposes of this book, we're only going to focus on Industrial Philosophy and how it helps the individual at work. Wise Up! For Teams and Wise Up! For Organizations come next on the horizon.

And since **self-knowledge is the most important knowledge**, let's start with you.

I Kant Do It!

That's not a typo. I had to throw in a nerdy philosopher pun - forgive me. Immanuel Kant was a German Prussian philosopher during the Age of Enlightenment.

Kidding about Kant aside, he believed in something important. This idea is so important - so important - I want you to agree with me on it before we go even further.

If you are outright closed to this, you might have a little trouble with all of the other concepts and ideas presented in this book. I'm not trying to pressure you right out of the gate, and usually, I'm a huge fan of questioning everything before I accept or reject ideas. But I'm emphasizing that it's critical you at least consider this notion. Immanuel Kant (and many others) believed that:

Your mind shapes and structures your experiences.

It's really true and hard to deny that if you believe you can't do something, you probably can't do it.

I should know. It happened to me.

A Funny Thing Happened to Me on the Way to a Status Meeting

You'll never believe how industrial philosophy can help a panic attack.

When this wisdom hit me, I was working in a senior position in advertising and marketing. My position came with a lot of stress, and I developed anxiety, along with all the unhealthy accouterments that come with it.

Every day - and in fact, several moments of every day - I faced a never-ending cycle of circling thoughts, and I was almost too paralyzed to get anything done. *I can't do anything right, I'm an imposter, I'll never get ahead*...these wayward thoughts and many others tormented my waking (and sleeping) hours. These thoughts also negatively impacted my performance. My presentations were never fully realized, my outputs were haphazard and shoddy, I missed deadlines, and I wasn't able to communicate clearly.

So, it's no surprise that after a while of existing this way, I had my first panic attack. On my way to a status meeting, no less.

And by status, I mean, regular, weekly, boring, nothing special about it meeting. I didn't have a major presentation, I wasn't pitching a multimillion-dollar client, and I wasn't meeting with the Pope. It was a no-big-deal meeting, the kind executives and employees everywhere experience all the time.

In the grand scheme of everything, **the meeting meant absolutely nothing.**

But my mind had been wrapped so tight in viciously sharp barbs of circling thoughts that it triggered a panic attack.

And it was the real deal - heart racing, vision fading to black and falling against the side of the hallway - **panic attack**. At the time, I was very aware that something was wrong, so I began to breathe deeply.

I felt very shaky and light-headed, but I also felt that I could not, *would not*, let on to anyone that anything was wrong, and I had to not only get through this meeting, but I had to make my status update anyway. So, I took small, baby steps all the way from my desk down to the conference room, and I sat down, put on a brave face and acted outwardly as though everything was fine, but inside, I could feel my heart palpitating a thousand beats per minute.

I don't even remember what happened in the meeting - just that somehow, I presented the status update. Afterward, I made my way back to my desk, and I calmed myself down to get the rest of my work done for the day.

Later that night, I researched my symptoms, and I discovered that I had, indeed, experienced a panic attack. That knowledge floored me. I knew I had been feeling stressed out, but I could not believe that I had actually suffered a panic attack.

That was my wake-up call.

I Can't Believe an Assassinated Dead Guy Would Save My Life

This panic attack occurred around the exact same time I was taking introductory philosophy classes. During these night adult education classes, I learned how my mind and thoughts actually worked.

I was absolutely horrified by the discovery of how cluttered my thoughts actually were.

Gradually, over time, **I applied the philosophical principles I studied to actual situations at work**. Ideas from Socrates, Ficino, Epictetus, Emerson, Allen, and countless others. I saw more clearly and observed what was actually happening at work. I was able to understand what was in my control and what was out of my control.

Then Things Got Real

I developed a more realistic view of what was *really* going on around me. The relationships I had at work improved, and I felt better about them. I connected more, and I was also able to put forth more ideas, as opposed to feeling burdened by everything and alienated from everyone.

I began to achieve a level of success I hadn't experienced or so fully been present for in the past - such as starting a new department at The New York Times.

But the real achievement for me wasn't the title or the new role. **It was my new-found ability to work effortlessly.** It was being able to go in and do what I needed to do and be able to work without pressure, even though I was consistently immersed in pressure cooker situations from the time I got in the office until I walked out the door.

And the bigger truth? I became healthier, and no sequel panic attack occurred.

I also began regularly applying philosophy in my management role, in how I related and guided employees and partners, and I started to see benefits here, too. During this time, one employee told me **I was the best boss she ever had**, and to me, that's a serious accolade, as most people experience perhaps one good boss, if that, in their entire careers. Even my bosses started coming to me for advice.

From implementing philosophy into my work, I developed a style of leadership that comes from wisdom. This approach resonated with both employees and colleagues. Things started to feel a lot better, and therefore work got a lot better. This "better" state of work stayed strong, even if it wasn't perfect and even if every situation remained quite challenging and less than ideal.

I was able to be okay with it, warts and all. Because of that, I was able to see more for myself.

The result is the book you're holding in your hands right now.

Imagine yourself or your employees being able to transcend these kinds of impediments and sustain this approach to work in a long-lasting way.

To excel, create, ideate, or just to have things roll off your back.

What's Going on in Your Mind According to Philosophy

Your mind influences to a very large degree, how you see the world and how you feel about it. Those things you say to yourself, in those darkest moments, are shaping your reality.

I repeat: those thoughts shape how you perceive reality.

And here's where we need to agree (or agree to disagree) that it's entirely possible that those thoughts and ideas that you have about what you think reality is might not always be true.

So, if it's possible that your thoughts are just passing things that aren't always rooted in truth or reality, that they are only an interpretation from your reactions and your mind, based on past experiences or future anxieties, they might just be impacting how you experience work.

If you are your own worst critic at work, you likely feel anxious about how well you're doing. You're caught up in people's opinions of you, and every little nuance of a conversation gets blown up in your mind to prove you right. Doesn't work, then, feel like a gauntlet or look like one? That's because you've convinced yourself that it is.

Your mind is ground zero for most of the experiences in your life. Your experiences can be looked at as neither good nor bad, or they can be looked at as all bad, or they could be looked at as all good.

But here's the thing: declaring something as good or bad is a judgment. It's your mind trying to make sense of and categorize what is in front of you.

The biggest obstacle to change, especially when it comes to thoughts and mindset, is really your perception of those thoughts and your judgment of those thoughts. The activities of the mind, the chatter, the noise, the flight or fight.

The biggest obstacle to you doing the work or having a great work life is the thoughts in your mind.

If you were to go back to that list of thoughts that I had in The Biggest Crisis Facing the World of Work, and you were to actually sit down and ask yourself: are they true? Is that what's really happening? Am I sure? Could there be something else I'm not seeing?

Am I clear on my knowledge, reality, and existence at work, or am I making up stories in my head about it?

If you ask questions about your thoughts, you begin to observe those thoughts in a more objective way. You might find there could be another way to look at things, which is part of the work that we're going to do - just finding another way to look at things.

Finding the truth.

This Is the Air Above the Tip of the Iceberg

There are, in my experience, hundreds of philosophical principles and practices. I've tried almost all of them (and I'm still discovering more!). I've hit the books, taken years of classes, and read original texts and passages from sages past. I've also perused scholarly articles, had deep conversations with philosophers and leaders, and gone diving deep into the mission and methodology of organizational change.

Last but not least, I've also lived good (and bad) management practices from the front lines.

From all of this experience, information, and insight, I have organized a primer for how to use philosophy in the workplace, so this is a great place to start. We're only seeing the tip of the iceberg here.

This is a get-started guide to wisdom for the workplace.

I've boiled it down to four aspects that will form our process:

- Clarity.
- Thoughts.
- Decisions.
- Actions.

My aim is to help you strengthen your abilities in each of those four tenets.

Even if you think you've got a handle on these, I guarantee there's more you can achieve.

What I've curated for you are the simplest, most straightforward ways that you can increase your clarity, have productive feelings and thoughts, decide what's right in every situation, and move towards action.

As I said before, your mind shapes your reality. It's also the other way around. Sometimes it's critical to put your mind to good use (reason) and also let the truth of a situation (reality) influence your mind. **And if your mind is constantly in fast forward mode or rewind mode - you're not going to feel grounded in either reality or reason.** Yikes!

What we're trying to do is hit the reset button, the stop button, or the pause button for just a certain amount of time - just enough so that you have the right amount of time to have the proper thoughts about a situation so that you know the right way to act.

Who wouldn't want that ability at work? Who wouldn't want that ability as a manager or a leader? It's entirely possible, to be able to change how you think and make your circumstances feel better.

Nothing about this process will force you to be something you're not. Nothing about this process is about, for example, compelling you to be happy if you're experiencing feelings of unhappiness. As a matter of fact, it encourages you to observe when you are unhappy so you can rise above it, as opposed to attaching to the unhappiness and giving up.

Everything about this process takes practice though, and I'm going to teach you how to go from being wise to acting wise.

The philosophers you're going to meet in this book really wanted what was best for you. They dedicated their lives, and some sadly gave their lives, because they wanted people to understand they were empowered.

The Corporate Holy Grail

"For whatever a great person does, others imitate. People conform to the standard which they have set." - Bhagavad Gita Ch. 3:21

Be the Standard

At work, people are watching. **They're looking to you to set the tone**. They're observing you for cues on the right way to act. If you're a leader and you want your teams and your organizations to listen to you, then you need to know your standards of what great is.

This actually starts with your mind and possessing a complete understanding of yourself.

Sometimes, though, when you're trying to accomplish more productive things like the   actual understanding of yourself, **your mind begins hijacking your time.**

Many people struggle daily with the sense that they're strapped for time, they're constantly seeking fulfillment, and they're often mired in the friction or downright conflict in work relationships. Most people yearn to do something better, and they seek to do the right thing at work.

Peace of Mind Costs Nothing and Impacts Everything

The right thing to do could be many things, and therein lies the challenge for a lot of people. Boiling it all down, **I believe we're all searching for peace of mind.** Peace of mind is the ability to sleep at night, to look ourselves in the mirror, and to be okay with what we see.

What if it's possible, even in the toughest situations, to have peace of mind? What would that be worth to you?

To at least be able to manage the here and now.

My hope is despite your circumstance, you can have peace of mind. A level of discernment and detachment that allows you to deal with the work at hand and move beyond it if that's your desire.

Or, to take a good situation and make it better.

If you think about just impacting your own working sphere, let's say you feel a little bit better about what you're doing and how you're doing it. That, in turn, influences the people around you. And let's just say, because of that, they're having a little bit of a better day at work, and they influence the people around them. Then all of a sudden you have a larger group of people who are operating from principle, values, and wisdom.

Then, you get a whole culture.

Then, you get a whole organizational model.

Then, you get a whole organizational way of existing and interacting with the world.

The Human in Human-Centered Organizations

I hear many leaders talk about purpose-driven organizations, healthy cultures, and so on. You can't really get to those things without really understanding this one idea: what purpose actually is (**hint: it's based** on principle), and what it is to actually be human (**hint: it's not your title, status, salary, or how busy you are**).

What I've seen is how philosophy answers those two things: defining principles and getting to the root of what makes us human. Truly understanding principles and human beings will allow your organization to connect with people and with your customers in a fundamental, universal way that maybe no other organization or employee engagement initiative can.

For people know and feel wisdom when they see it.

People know and feel truth when they experience it.

Pausing Off the Ledge

I know a financial advisor, who was a classmate of mine at philosophy school, who had been getting **frantic phone calls from his investors** because of a bad week in the market, due to the fears around the coronavirus. He told me how he had clients who were on the ledge when they called. He realized he needed to calm them down before they made any rash decisions.

So what did he do? **He asked them to pause: with him, one minute, over the phone.** He asked them to sit with him in a quiet moment of pausing, of complete silence. Then, they talked about the situation, and he was able to explain, and they were able to listen, that their finances were actually okay, based on how much they had earned over the years. This advisor told me how he did that with a lot of his skittish clients, and despite the market being in freefall, he said it **turned out to be an easy week.**

What he did was practice what you will learn in the chapter on Action.

Imagine what your work would feel like if that happened.

In addition, it's worth understanding that wisdom and maybe practicing philosophy at work actually works. Because, to be frank, it's stuff you already know and to some extent maybe you weren't really applying it or practicing it consistently.

Remember, wisdom is innate. These are things that are already inside of you. All we're doing is developing the skills to bring that forth to raise your level of understanding of the true nature of your knowledge reality and existence, and the true nature of your organization's knowledge reality and existence.

If that is achieved, you're operating on a whole other level.

Isn't that worth it?

Yes, Wisdom Can be Practical. Here's How.

Philosophy teaches us how to observe our minds and emotions so we can act wisely. **Philosophy is meant to be lived, used, and applied.** It is not meant to only be taken out when your yoga mat is unfolded or when your life is perfectly in tune with the universe.

In each of the following chapters, I'll present something that you can actually practice at work. Before presenting you with these actual practices, it's worth taking a quick moment to understand what it means to practice and why it's important.

It's one thing to have the knowledge of something, and quite another to have the experience of it.

You've seen this, you know the difference between someone who's speaking from a place that's maybe theoretical or academic, and someone who's got a really juicy story to tell about something that actually happened to them.

Who are you more engaged with? Who are you more likely to listen to? So when you practice philosophy and you practice the things that I'm going to teach you in this book, you begin to develop stories and observations of the things that happen. What that means is, this wisdom becomes a part of how you think and, more importantly, act.

How to Handle Conflict Philosophy Style

I once got very territorial with a colleague. I felt threatened and made the infantile decision to not loop them in as much as I probably should have. Unfortunately, we also worked in an environment that didn't much care about team dynamics so we continued to be at odds for quite a bit. One day, it all boiled over, and both of us were pretty upset with each other.

My colleague was ready to march to our boss's office and make a complaint. That's when I remembered this principle of unity, to observe how everything is connected, so I said, "Perhaps we don't need to separate further by drawing more distinctions between us, perhaps we need to be in each other's work even more?" This person looked at me, and I could see the truth of what I was saying reflected in their eyes.

I suggested we meet weekly for a coffee to talk about whatever we wanted. I suggested that we each share everything we were working on, and that we needed to be more attached at the hip than ever before. My colleague was game, and we tried it out. Things definitely got better. Our collaboration and conversations improved, and things became more relaxed.

Now, because of this tool and my experience of using it to resolve conflict, especially when it came to possessiveness and competition, I always remember how effective it is because I experienced it first hand.

Experience is like Mainlining Wisdom

When you move forward and you continue to practice your philosophy through your work, you will always remember the benefit of actually having tried this stuff out. This practice then becomes a part of who you are, and it becomes a part of the way that you work.

What we're trying to achieve here is a level of where **acting wise just becomes natural for you.**

Once you begin to embody who a wiser person is, who a wiser manager is, you begin to see the many ways you can have impact.

The best way to try these practices is just to try them out. Don't worry about whether you're doing it right, or if you're doing it wrong. All you're trying to find is an observation, all you're seeking is an experience.

This is where it usually becomes quite difficult for people so I'm going to challenge you to just grow your powers of observation. A lot of people question whether observing things actually makes a difference, and many of them have told me some version of this: "Well, then, I observed this thing happen so now what? What do I do with it?"

Believe it or not, there's really nothing for you to do other than to be aware - **to grow your awareness,** if you will. And that's really hard in this day and age because a lot of people strongly and stridently believe that they have to *do* something, *do* anything. And what I'm saying is no, actually, you don't.

The awareness, the observation, that is the work.

It is practicing philosophy. Observation is the linchpin of being a wise person. For some of you this sounds really compelling. For others, it's a big step, because you're not used to it. Yet you know you would be happier not always feeling like you have to have it figured out, or to always have to fix things or yourself. You can just let things be what they are.

A Few Tips

- I find post it notes and calendar reminders to be incredibly helpful when I'm practicing.

- I try to practice in conjunction with something else, like a cup of coffee.

- Meetings are a really great place to practice. So, before you go into a meeting, hold these ideas in mind, and see what happens.

The point is to find a way to remember to try these things out, to just do it. And don't worry about it if you don't get to it, and don't fret over it if you forget to do it. Just keep trying.

Charting Our Course

Here's a snapshot of what you're going to learn in the
next chapters.

Clarity	Thoughts	Decisions	Action
Desire for Truth	You Are Not Your Thoughts	Decisions are the Product of Fair and Reasonable Thought	Action and Non-Action Serve Each Other
✓ What is true? ✓ Look without opinion ✓ See as if for the first time	✓ Despite your thoughts, what is the work?	✓ Note the basis for your decisions ✓ Cultivate fairness, kindness, and truth ✓ Say "I don't know"	✓ Be of service ✓ Notice your environment ✓ What am I valuing now?

Clarity: Know Before You No

"True power is sitting back and observing things with logic." - Warren Buffet

Have any of these happened to you?

- You've just said something in a meeting, but all you're getting is blank stares.

- You walked away from a conversation, and something about that interaction didn't feel right.

- You're getting emails every time you blink, and your eyes glaze over.

- You are pretty sure you know exactly what that person is going to say and how they're going to say it, and how they're going to act, every time.

Are you paying attention? Do you actually know what's in front of you, really know what is there? Can you see what's going on around you?

We are in the realm of the real now.

Your senses are the front lines of perceiving what's actually going on around you. But in order to actually experience and process reality, you will have to **bypass your knee-jerk responses, and tap into a more reasoned mind** and allow it to interpret what your senses are experiencing.

That's what having clarity is all about.

How many times have you made a snap judgement about a situation - but you were totally wrong about what was going on?

That person didn't hate your presentation - **she was just worried about her sick grandma.**

Your team totally gets what you're saying - **they're just hungover from the Christmas party.**

The CEO isn't mad at your employee's comment - **they're just hangry because they skipped breakfast.**

If you understand what's really going on around you, if you perceive properly, you'll be working off of the most accurate information available to you. Isn't that important?

The Reality Check

How do we start anything worth doing? We start from principle.

So, we need to start from a principle about clarity, and that principle is **"we have a desire for truth."**

In a lot of ways, this is something that is inherent almost in our DNA. For if we do not understand the truth of a situation, if we aren't grounded in what's real, we could put ourselves in danger - fall off a cliff, eat a poisonous mushroom, or get eaten by a saber tooth tiger (you know, back in the day). We all have a desire for truth.

We see this a lot in the working world. People call it transparency, honesty, radical candor.

I call it *the Truth*.

Because all of those other things - transparency, honesty, and radical candor - are reconfigured definitions of the truth, and the truth is filtered through the lens of someone else's perspective. What I'm saying is there's only, *the Truth*, and your job is to get to as close to that, without opinion and without judgment, as you possibly can.

To get as close to it as you can without anyone else's opinions, without anyone else's noise, and without anyone else's chatter.

What Do You Desire Most?

Unless I'm mistaken, you probably prefer to have people tell you the truth. I'm pretty certain you don't like it when people lie to you, or when the vendor across the table fudges their promises to get the sale, or when an employee continues to dance around something that happened. There's something inside of you that gets irritated by these deceptions and deceits.

By and large people are predisposed to desire, seek, and want the truth.

Some of you are sighing. "Now, Cristina, I know this might be true in an ideal world, but in the real world where I work, most people lie, or deceive, or outright ignore the truth. The truth hurts."

No, I'm saying, this is still true. **People prefer the truth.** They really do. While it's very likely that you might know several people within your life whom you see as promoting distortions and dishonesty, if you took a closer look at things, you might see this very different picture I'm presenting you.

What often happens is people's perceptions about the truth - their opinions and judgments about situations, people, and results - cloud what is their very real desire for the truth.

Sunk in the Unreal

A very real example of this is "sunk-costs" thinking. You have a project or department that's failing or hemorrhaging money, time, and resources, but because you've spent so much time, effort, and money on this thing, you refuse to admit or see that it's not working. To add to that, people - either employees, clients, or leadership - are unhappy, and on some level, they all know the truth. But they hang on, way past the point of reason, simply because they don't want to acknowledge the truth.

It's important at work to have a desire for truth and to know that the place from which you're operating functions as clearly as possible. How can you work well if you're working off faulty information? One important thing to keep in mind is that we mostly operate from our ideas about what is true, and those ideas are based on our own biases and past experiences.

We're not always aware of what's actually true.

Consider the times you thought a situation was one way when it actually wasn't - and not because of unknown factors- but because you weren't paying attention or you applied your own filter on it. This happens all the time.

So many times, I would take my team, and we would meet with our clients in a conference room, and in the middle of pitching our campaign to them, I would start looking at them, and I was absolutely, positively sure that they *hated* our presentation. I just knew they didn't like what we were saying at all, but then, in a day or two, or even, sometimes immediately after the presentation, they'd tell us they loved it.

Or, there also were times when my team and I would make our pitch to a client, in a similar conference room, and after we were done, I was so sure we nailed it, so sure that this would be our next big client...and then, we weren't hired, or our client didn't like our campaign so we had to go back to the drawing board.

And then, there were times, when my team and I would make our presentation, again, in a similar conference room, and as we made our pitch, I couldn't tell if our clients loved our ideas or hated them, and then I started wondering, worrying, if we were doing something wrong, because I couldn't discern their emotions about our presentation, and before our presentation was even finished, my mind was already obsessing and starting to panic.

Good, bad, or neutral, in each of these cases, my thoughts about the experience were not the truth of the experience. In fact, my thoughts were hindering me and preventing me from seeing and knowing what actually was going on.

These days there's a lot of talk about dealing with ambiguity - about how to deal with it, how to make decisions in such an ambiguous environment, and so on. But to me, ambiguity is mostly about not knowing the future outcome or the consequences of something. It's not about actually knowing the truth of a situation or what's in front of you. That's actually available to you anytime, and I'll show you how to determine this.

All you have to do is **look without opinion.**

All you have to do is **ask one question.**

All you have to do is **see the everyday as if for the first time.**

Do that, and you have the world in your sights.

Speaking the Truth

If you're not yet convinced, continue on, and read what these philosophers said about Truth. Take one that resonates with you and consider it more fully.

"No pleasure is comparable to the standing upon the vantage ground of truth."
— Francis Bacon

"The world is full of magic things, patiently waiting for our senses to grow sharper." — W.B. Yeats

"There are
things known
and there are
things unknown,
and in between
are the doors of
perception." —
Aldous Huxley

"It is one thing to show a man that he is in error, and another to put him in possession of truth." — John Locke

"How sweet is the perception of a new natural fact!" - Henry David Thoreau

"The questions which one asks oneself begin, at least, to illuminate the world, and become one's key to the experience of others." - James Baldwin

Truth Takeaways

What I believe these philosophers are offering is:

- The truth is ever-present, waiting to be seen.

- Being truthful, or at one with the truth, provides serenity.

- Being right does not mean proving someone wrong.

- The path to knowing starts with questioning yourself.

Make No Mistake

I'm making a big claim here, but my experience is the closer you get to the Truth or reality as a basis of your approach to work, the chances of making big mistakes or having big misunderstandings decreases.

Based on the principle of "We have a desire for truth," you can practice this at work. In any situation, the truth of a moment can be made available to you, and here's how you can perceive it:

Truth Practice

Look without opinion: When you are in a situation or a conversation, when you are digesting information or creating something, look at it for what it is. Take in just the essential sensory facts - what it looks like, what it sounds like, where you are, how you are sitting, etc. Do not form an idea, an opinion, or a judgement about it. Let that person say what they're saying, hear the words. Let the meeting unfold in front of you, observe who's in the room and what is happening. Don't get out of the moment by anticipating what's going to happen next or judging the situation before it completely unfolds. (For you mindfulness folks, this one's for you!)

Ask the question "What is true at this moment?": You've been given information, some good news or maybe some bad news. Or you just had a thought about your own performance, or perhaps you received some criticism. This is an excellent time to ask yourself: *What is true at this moment?* or *Is this true?* This very question may trigger an answer. That answer could be a truth worth noting. Just observe the situation, the fact that you asked the question, and note what the answer was. Do not let other noise interject on what you are assessing as the truth at the moment.

Meet the situation or the person as new every time.
Before you do that performance review, before you
work on version gazillion.10 of that presentation, and
definitely before you think you know the situation,
pretend for one moment that you are seeing that
person, that output, or that situation as if for the very
first time. Pretend as if everything before didn't exist.
Now, look at this situation, output, or person with fresh
eyes.

I "Need It Now" Version

I get it. This can be heady stuff. You might already be thinking it's too much to remember. Perhaps you realize that you're not ready to delve into changing things just yet. And you probably want something quick that you can try out in a pinch.

Whatever the case may be, I'm going to give you the "Need It Now" version. In other words, a practice when you need something right away (even though I think the others serve just as well for those times, too).

So here's what you do to ensure that you're seeing the Truth right now, right away:

Question your first reaction.

That's it. Every reaction you have for the next few days, do not trust it, and do not act on it. Ask what is the reaction all about or why are you reacting that way?

The most important thing to keep in mind with these exercises is that *the observation* is the work.

Observing yourself practicing is part of applying wisdom.

There's nothing "to do" so refrain from trying to have to do anything about it or figure anything out. That adds pressure, and that's completely unnecessary.

The practicing is the "doing" part.

As I mentioned in the chapter of "Yes, Wisdom Can be Practical" try these exercises for one week. Set reminders or ways that you can remember this as your practice so that you actually can experience them in action at work. Figure out a way to incorporate the practice with another activity, such as a meeting or morning coffee, so that you remember it. The more you practice, the easier it will be for you to take yourself out of things and see things as they are.

The Grains of Truth

As you practice and become more observant, and the truth reveals itself in clear and concrete ways, **you may experience an increase in confidence, security, peace,**

or assurance. You may even recognize there's nothing that needs to be done or that you don't need to affect anything. You can sit in observatory mode, allowing a situation to do the work of informing you without you needing to do anything.

This allows you to determine and focus your thoughts on what's important.

Your days, then, become more about thinking of the bigger picture, coming up with ways to innovate, establishing better relationships at work with your team, and making your mark.

My work with executives often encompasses discussing philosophical concepts and practicing them at work.

Here are some of the astonishing things that have happened to my clients after they viewed seeing the truth in their work.

"If someone was wrong, it was my obligation to make sure they knew that they were wrong. With this practice, I learned that it's okay for someone else to be wrong as long as it's not going to cause death. So when I thought about the sentence 'It is one thing to show a man he is an error,' I stopped trying to convince people they're wrong, and maybe allow them to come to the conclusion that they're wrong on their own because then, they're a lot more in a belief about that. They'll actually do something about it." -- **Director of Sales, Consulting Firm**

"I felt different when I really knew the truth about something, and someone was trying to convince me otherwise, to tell me something that is untrue. It's so different now when I know the truth about a situation, I see when someone feeds me a line of BS about it. It's very calming to know the truth. Instead of having to make a judgment on whether what they're saying is true or not true, I don't have to do that." - **VP of Communications, Advertising Agency**

"I did the observe-without-labeling thing. In a meeting, I just sat back and watched. Usually, I'm the first person to kick things off and talk through what needs to be done. Instead, I just said, "Anyone want to start?" And I sat back and watched the team go. I saw them talk, share, get things done. This feeling of 'Wow, this is a great team!' came over me. At first, I kept wanting to jump in and say something, but I remembered to just observe, and then I felt ok and relaxed a bit. I actually didn't need to do much of anything. I can't help but think: how many times in the past have I taken over too much? Now, I'm thinking I may do that again. I think they liked me not butting in all the time." - **Marketing Strategist, Publishing Company**

On Thinking: The Good, The Bad, The Ugly

"You will continue to suffer if you have an emotional reaction to everything that is said to you." - Warren Buffet

Though Warren Buffet is obviously wise, I've worked with people who still operate against this principle.

"Why can't they have a thought, any thought?" my boss once asked me about a particular employee. Quiet people made my boss nervous. Maybe my boss felt it was a sign of a lack of motivation or ambition, or perhaps it represented something inside my boss that they didn't want to see in themselves.

In any event, my boss went from thought to opinion to judgment in 60 seconds flat.

However, the actual truth was my employee was introverted, and this amazing, introverted employee had just delivered a spectacular presentation in the previous week, a rockstar performance if I've ever seen one, and in fact, my boss had been in attendance to this. But the quiet unnerved my boss so much that a whole bunch of thoughts were spun around this employee and my boss's judgment of the employee. My boss didn't see the truth for what it was - that my employee was exceptional, just reserved.

Don't Go to Last Week's Meeting

Another time, I had a colleague whose favorite idea for an ad campaign concept got shot down in a meeting. This idea was their absolutely *favorite* idea. And even though one of their other, lesser favorite ideas was greenlit with very little changes, they stewed about their favorite idea getting trampled.

I ran into them again, a week later, and they were still stewing about what happened!

They were still in that meeting, still attached to their idea, and still having a hard time moving forward with the work on the actual, approved concept, which was a solid concept which the client loved. But they couldn't let this one idea go.

Needless to say, from this point on, the project became a slog for everyone. Even worse, the client noticed the change in the energy and attitude, and what could have been an energizing, fun project became a burden. And it didn't have to be this way.

Did They Just Say 'Tampon'?

I once watched a senior vice president put a new employee on the spot on their very first day, and ask them to give their opinion on an entire advertising campaign that had been months in the making. I had worked with this SVP for years so I knew their approach was to make sure people could "hit the ground running." Though clearly uncomfortable, the pressure to provide a thought, any thought, was so great the new hire stammered out feedback that wasn't thoughtful. Some of it was downright insulting ('This creative looks like an ad for tampons," was one comment. I kid you not.) This thoughtless feedback helped no one, least of all, the creative directors who practically died to make this campaign happen. Everyone was scowling, except, of course, the SVP, who thought they were doing the right thing but instead ended up damaging the goodwill of the entire team.

These situations reveal a great truth: Is it that important to constantly be in thought? Can we get too attached to our ideas and thoughts? With this pressure to have ideas, pronouncements, and opinions all the time, aren't we diluting and degrading our ability to distinguish productive thinking versus those thoughts which are detrimental? And what is the downside of all of this thinking and overthinking all of the time?

You know yourself when you've seen your own thoughts run away from you. Perhaps you're like that colleague of mine, still ruminating over what happened in last week's meeting while the clock is ticking on the deadline looming in front of you.

Or, maybe, you're **scrambling to speak up in a meeting** to impress your client when you really don't have anything that important to say. That's why they furrow their brow when you're speaking, because you're not saying anything that makes sense.

Or, you are so focused on that big project that hasn't even happened yet that **you can't sleep at night**.

Sometimes, all of this thinking isn't productive at all - it's downright harmful. Just having a thought, forcing an issue, or holding steadfast to an opinion might not be helpful.

If You're Happy and You Know it, Overthink

This thinking is so habitual that we don't even realize what's going on in our heads. For example, how many times have you sat in a meeting, and then you caught your employee looking at you. **"Oh, they gave me a look in this meeting. What is that all about?"** you ask yourself. And it's not even that they gave you a nasty look, they just looked at you, but your thoughts and feelings about that look made the look nasty.

So, after the meeting, you're sitting there, thinking about this employee, wondering what that look was all about and whether she was going to get her project done on time, and then, you start wondering if they're up to the task. But instead of just following up and asking them if they're okay, you continue to think about that look.

The wise thing to do is to go and investigate it, but a lot of times, people won't do anything about it. They just sit with this thought, and they create a whole other reality about this thought, and they don't even know if this reality exists or not.

If you actually asked your employee, they might tell you that they're fish died, or that they needed more coffee, or that they weren't thinking anything bad at all, they just forgot to wear their glasses that morning and were actually squinting at the white board behind you.

This practice of forced thinking - or circular thinking or habitual thinking - can keep us stuck.

Now, not all thoughts are bad, but there's a distinct difference between the thoughts that go nowhere and keep us going nowhere, and the thoughts that lead to clarity and productivity.

Circular thinking comes from telling ourselves a story that we've created in our heads about a person or a situation, and we keep thinking this same thing, over and over and over, and it goes nowhere and nowhere good.

Productive thinking, on the other hand, leads to a positive or forward moving outcome. It has a direction, it definitely goes somewhere, and it isn't repetitive.

Productive thinking is inspired thinking, and when you are experiencing an inspired thought, you can definitely feel it.

Have you ever had a situation where you *felt* an idea or *felt* a thought? And it felt right. It felt true. You just sort of knew what to do, you knew how you felt about it, and sometimes you felt really strongly about it. Something was presented, and your immediate thought was "That's the thing. That's the answer. That's the right idea."

What's actually going on is you are having an inspired idea about what's right and true. If you're aware enough that a thought felt true, you were actually having an appropriate thought, an appropriate feeling, or an appropriate reaction, to something.

Now I know that sounds really dry and boring, but this is where you can get tripped up. A lot of times, our thoughts and our feelings drive many of the things we do and the decisions we make.

But here's the catch: If we do not completely trust our thoughts and feelings and where they're coming from, or if we are not aware of our actual thoughts and feelings and where they're coming from, everything else is going to be colored through those thoughts and feelings. **And these are the kinds of thoughts, feelings, and reactions that *are not true*.**

In the working world, thoughts and feelings such as *this person wants to do my job*, *I had a bad day and everything sucks*, or any of those other existential thoughts and feelings that we talked about before, will cloud your ability to see things as they are and to actually determine your own thoughts and feelings.

What we want to develop is your ability to determine what you think, meaning you as in YOU - not your title, not your status, not the ideas of you or your work.

Your reasoned mind.

The reasoning YOU, not the you that's afraid, not the you that's worried. The real you. We're using reason to understand how you truly feel about something.

You Are Not A Pen

The principle for the practices around Thoughts is - ***you are not your thoughts.***

Let me repeat this principle: *you are not your thoughts.*

By now, you are beginning to recognize that your feelings and thoughts shape your reality, or your perception of your reality, and those thoughts impact your ability to deal with your external circumstances. **This principle is saying that all those thoughts you are having aren't actually who you are.** They're just thoughts. They might be true, and they might not be true. They are just thoughts that are flitting through your brain at a particular moment in time.

One thing to keep in mind, while these ideas are saying that your thoughts impact your reality, they are not proposing you are only thoughts. That's like saying you have a thought about a pen, then you must be a pen! So if you are not a pen, then what are you?

You are wise, my friend, you are *that who sees the pen*. I feel like I sound like Morpheus from The Matrix here.

The more that you put those circling thoughts under observation, the more you examine those thoughts and question those thoughts, the more you will be able to **determine the difference between a thought or feeling that is appropriate and one that's coming from, maybe another place, such as fear, nervousness, agitation, rashness, hurriedness, competitiveness, or restlessness.**

What we're looking for here is not to downplay your feelings or to downplay your thoughts. But what we're trying to do is to stabilize your relationship with them and to stabilize your ability to distinguish the difference between a thought and a feeling that feels really true and one that's coming from a place that isn't true.

That is why *you are not your thoughts* is a really important principle.

Hold That Thought

The ideas and concepts offered by these philosophers center around the choice of our thoughts leading to the quality of our thoughts.

Thoughts are impermanent things. They move, they come and go. Sometimes they're random, and sometimes they're sticky (the thoughts like 'Why did I just think of that presentation I did three years ago? or 'I can't shake replaying that meeting in my head') but they are NOT you, they are not who you truly are.

They only inform, advise, debate, contradict, make unreal your external circumstances.

Which is also to say that you are NOT your external circumstances either. Do you really think you are your title, salary, or role, and that's all you are? Maybe you feel like you're just an ATM machine giving out money to employees, vendors, and such. I get it.

But I have some exciting news for you, **you are a way higher order than all of that.**

You recognizing this is the real reason for this book.

Before we get into your practices around quality Thoughts, let's contemplate what great minds have to say about having a great mind.

"You have free will about the attitude you bring in." - Epictetus

"While there is only one thing we can care about and attach ourselves to, we choose instead to care about and attach ourselves to a score of others: to our bodies, to our property... And, being attached to many things, we are weighed down and dragged along with them. If the weather keeps us from traveling, we sit down and fret. What should we do then? Make the best use of what is in our power and treat the rest in accordance with nature." - Epictetus, Discourses 1:1: 14

"It is not what happens to us that disturbs us but what we think about what happens to us." - Epictetus

"Beware the barrenness of a busy life." - Socrates

"The human brain is a complex organ with the wonderful power of enabling a man to find reasons for continuing to believe whatever it is that he wants to believe." - Voltaire

"As long as a man stands in his own way, everything seems to be in his way."
- Ralph Waldo Emerson

"In order to go on living, one must try to escape the death involved in perfectionism."- Hannah Arendt

Fighting the Trojan Thoughts

What's offered here in these passages are:

- You are more in control than you think you are.

- Busyness of mind is not fulfilling, even though it may appear that way.

- We can have a host of attachments, and this often causes misery.

- We can get stuck in our belief of something.

Why do these concepts matter at work?

A lot of times we feel we're being batted around at work by meetings, demands, pressure, competition, and striving. Taking a closer look, though, is it possible that the meetings, demands, pressure, competition, and striving are creations of our minds acting out and reacting to what we think is happening?

When we get tired, frustrated, and feel helpless, often we may feel a barrenness to our jobs.

Let's say we begin to cling to these ideas and thoughts - that we're always busy, we're always under pressure, and so on. These thoughts and ideas become our sense of reality.

Unchecked, unexamined, or unchallenged, they then become our sense of ourselves. And then, we work from that place, we lead from that place, and if we have any ideas at all at this point, all of our ideas come from that place. It's like a Trojan Horse that entered into your mind and is spilling out.

Let's say you're on the hook to present ideas to make changes to your department. If you feel put upon, burdened, overwhelmed, or undervalued - how good do you think your ideas are going to be?

You might just do the minimum to get through the presentation. You may present "safe" ideas because you're worried about making waves, and you might even think that's what you want, that's what's good for you or your department. You won't stretch, you won't innovate, and you won't really progress because you're not coming from a place that thinks that's even possible.

Wow, things just got really dark for a second.

What if you weren't all of those things your mind is saying you are? What if you aren't actually overwhelmed, you just think you are?

Let's explore the possibility that if you set aside your thoughts (overwhelmed, undervalued, and so on) for one moment, what would be left?

The work.

That presentation.

And what's more important to deal with in the moment you have right now?

It's the Thought That Counts

In the spirit of helping you "get on with it" because that's the reality of your work and your life right now, here's an exercise I've used in the past when I was really in my head and struggling to get anything done.

I trained my mind to be less spin doctor and be more creative, in the space of the work, and to increase my focus and feel more in control.

Thought Practice

Practice: Despite your thoughts about it, what is the work that remains?

I can hear you gasping, clutching your heart maybe. Stay with me! We place a lot of emphasis on our identities at work, or how our work defines our identities. Sometimes the emphasis is so strong that it becomes an impediment to actually being able to complete our work or engage with it. Add to that, different roles and expectations in a group dynamic, and you will have situations where circling thoughts can keep you from having perspective and "getting on with it."

Your thoughts about the work aren't as important as the work itself. It's not that having thoughts is a bad thing; it's that your attachment to those thoughts can become a bad thing, or rather, an impediment to your work and your progress as a human being. Your attachment to your thoughts can keep you stuck.

So the practice is, when you're trying to get work done or that deadline is looming and you feel you're in that moment that you're hesitating or that you're spinning out, and you're not sure why - ask yourself, *What thoughts about the work are coming up right now?* Are they important to the work, or are they just ideas I'm having about the work? Am I in control, or are my thoughts in control right now? Observe what comes up.

I "Need It Now" Version

Here's what you do when you are spiraling in thoughts or can't get rid of your angst about a situation at work:

Tell yourself, "It's temporary."

That meeting sucked. *It's temporary.*

I can't figure this out. *It's temporary.*

I'm miserable working with this person. *It's temporary.*

It's temporary. It's temporary. It's temporary.

Whatever you're experiencing, *you* are not stuck in that moment; it's just your thoughts that are stuck. You will not exist in that permanent state of "this is f'ed up" because things will move on. To help your mind move on, redirect your activity to tackle a small task to help you feel like you accomplished something, to put your circling mind onto something else.

On Second Thought

Here are a few people who practiced this idea and here's what they observed.

"I became more conscious of when someone was talking or when something was going on, to be aware of what was happening, as opposed to having my mind wander off to something else and start multitasking. This used to happen to me when someone else was talking about a topic that wasn't as interesting to me. So with this practice, I became very aware of the fact that if somebody else was talking or doing something, that I try to stay more tuned in to what was going on as opposed to going off into other areas of interest. I was calmer as a result of this practice. I tried to stay more into the presence of what was going on, as opposed to being impatient and wanting to be engaged in other things or do other things when someone was talking to me about something that was important to them. Just because we're not doing what we want to do, that doesn't mean that what somebody else is talking to us about isn't important to them. I needed to listen to what others were saying, to stay tuned into what they were saying and not worry about all the other stuff I could be doing." **- Head of Employee Engagement, State Government**

"I had a presentation that had to do for a client, and I didn't think it went well, and I think it could have gone better. I began to realize I was in these thoughts, and I started to look at it as: what could I learn from the experience? In the moment, in the things that didn't go the way that I thought they could have gone, I asked myself: how can I stop and use this as a moment of teaching, rather than a moment of regret or missed opportunity?" - **Chief Strategy Officer, Advertising Agency**

"I had to present a big idea to the CRO of my company. It was work I really wanted to do, and I had put my heart and soul into this presentation. If they liked the idea, I could continue on with the work I wanted to do. If they didn't like it, I would be relegated to my previous role. I was very nervous as this CRO was extremely sharp and well regarded. I remembered the practice of "My thoughts about the work" and started to feel that my presentation was what was more important, meaning the idea itself and not me necessarily. I came to understand that the work was what was being judged, not me. It was strange because as I dissociated with my idea, I removed myself and my worries from it. This feeling of calm came over me. When I presented to the CRO, it was lovely! I wasn't as nervous as I thought I would be, and I felt I was able to explain my ideas more clearly, and I was able to engage with them in a more personable way. Needless to say, they were happy with what I was doing, and they let me continue on. But the

crazy thing was, I came to realize even if they didn't think the work should continue, it didn't have any bearing on who I was." - **Marketing Strategist, Publishing Company**

Decisions:
A State of
Independence

"If words control you, that means everyone else can control you." - Warren Buffet

I was sitting in my boss's office one day as we were doing a working session on a project, so I was there for a couple of hours. In that span of time, almost every 20 to 30 minutes, a different team member would interrupt our meeting to get a sign-off or ask for an opinion on something else. Every time this happened, my boss felt they had to make a call on that item, right on the spot. Everything - from the Christmas party's decorations to major hiring decisions - was equally urgent. This sense of urgency for everything created a very reactionary culture, and as a result, we could never get past first base on anything. People weren't empowered to do their work and move forward, and neither was my boss.

When was the last time you made a pros/cons list? Yet, we make decisions at work that would impact us for years to come without doing this simple task that really helps us decide what to do.

I think the whole rhetoric around **shooting from the hip or making decisions on the fly might be a neat justification we've made for ourselves to continue to feed the hamster wheel pace we're all now accustomed to.**

Typically, when we make those kinds of decisions, it's based on two things: what happened before, and what's going to happen to us as a result of said decision.

Are we doing the right thing, though? Are we making decisions that are in the best interest of us, our employees, and our organization? Are we taking the time to understand what is really influencing us?

Deliberation is the work of decision making, it's the whole process - of being able to think clearly and see things for what they really are. In this current working environment, where people are in back-to-back meetings, feeling totally overwhelmed, and wearing many hats, our ability to look, to deliberate, and to decide has been really compromised.

Our ability to make these decisions clearly is one of the most important things we can do in the world of work.

Yet as we're pressured to think fast and do more, we're encouraged to fail fast, in our highly competitive, outcome-driven environments.

Let's be honest: our ability and the **time we allow ourselves to deliberate over the right thing to do, has been impacted.**

Running on instinct is only a very small piece of the puzzle. Gut remains important, but so many people are running on autopilot, they're making uninformed decisions that negatively affect them, their employees, and their companies. People also make decisions by taking historical, past experiences and applying them to even new situations, which keeps them from innovating and trying anything new.

How often have you told yourself or your employees, "This is the way we've always done it."

Are you making critical decisions, with long-term consequences, on the fly without actually having developed your ability to deliberate? Are you making big decisions, without taking a moment to consider them? Or, something seemed simple and innocuous so you rattled off a response to just get it off your list, and it ended up blowing back up in your face?

In hindsight, you realize if you had given the situation even a teensy bit of attention, the consequences wouldn't have been so intense.

When the Bite-Size Bites Back

We're so busy and overloaded that we remain obsessed with moving onto the next thing as quickly and as painlessly as possible. To keep moving on that hamster wheel, we've become reliant on "bite-size" content. You know exactly what I'm talking about - those top ten lists written in content mills that have been SEO'd to death with barely any substance behind them at all. Or, those latest, pithy, buzzy statements from some management gurus who are probably using the exact same top ten lists themselves.

Why are we doing this? **Because our reactionary mind wants us to set it and forget it**, so it can move onto the next thing, because it's easier to look at a list and think we're actually doing something, then to actually take a hard look within ourselves.

We don't trust ourselves anymore to make the right decisions, and we've been trained by fear to avoid any possibility that something can go wrong. So, instead, we look to preformulated ideas from other people to make the decisions for us.

Or perhaps we're relying too much on the three-bullet executive summary that has oversimplified a sensitive or high-stakes situation.

What's the cost?

The cost is our independence, our very ability to think for ourselves.

If you want to innovate, if you truly want to lead, you have to have your own mind, you have to have your own ideas, and you have to use your own language. You can't do this if you're **"parroting other men's ideas,"** to paraphrase Ralph Waldo Emerson.

What I'm presenting to you in this chapter is for you to **hold sacred your independent thinking**. And you, deciding the right thing to do without influence, without doing what's been done before, will help you deliberate these very hard decisions you face every day.

Mind of Your Own

Somewhere deep inside, you know what to do. **You know what needs to be done.** In this day and age of focus grouping, satisfaction surveys, click-through-rate reports, have we opted out of seeing for ourselves? Do we not trust ourselves enough? Perhaps our attention is so compromised that we wouldn't know a good decision if it hit us over the head.

Or maybe, you know what to do, but you're afraid to do it. It won't make you popular, you won't be the cool boss, or you don't want to face the firing squad of questions so it's best to do what everyone else thinks is the best idea. That's fine, if **the best idea is actually based on what's true and good**, and it's not based on some faulty, whitewashed agenda.

So our principle for Decisions is that decisions are the product of fair and reasonable thought.

Luckily, there's some guidance around that we can lean on. I've selected a smattering of philosophers and concepts for this because I want you to see the full breadth of thoughts on this very important principle.

Let's take a moment and contemplate what's being offered in these passages. Then we'll practice how to properly decide.

Making Decisions is Easier than You Think

"In you is your best counselor - not men or books - your Inward Leader - enjoining the fit word and the fit act for every moment." - Ralph Waldo Emerson

"A man's mind may be likened to a garden, which may be intelligently cultivated or allowed to grow wild; but whether cultivated or neglected, it must and will bring forth. If no useful seeds are put into it, then an abundance of useless weed-seeds will fall thereon, and continue to produce their kind."
— James Allen

"The solution of the problem in life is seen in the vanishing of the problem." — Ludwig Wittgenstein

"Fair, kind, and true is all my argument." - Shakespeare, Sonnet 105

"To be a good human being is to have a kind of openness to the world, an ability to trust uncertain things." - Martha Nussbaum

"Doubt is an unpleasant condition, but certainty is absurd." — Voltaire

"Check yourself before you wreck yourself." — Ice Cube

"Then my friend, we must not regard what the many say of us: but what he, the one man who has understanding of just and unjust, will say, and what the truth will say. And therefore you begin in error when you advise that we should regard the opinion of the many about just and unjust, good and evil, honorable and dishonorable." - Dialogues of Plato, Crito 48a.

"I am wiser than this man, for neither of us appears to know anything great and good; but he fancies he knows something although he knows nothing; whereas I, as I do not know anything, so I do not fancy I do." - Socrates

Getting Good at Good Decisions

The passages above illustrate that we:

- Have the capacity to cultivate our minds to deliberate.

- That the perception of a problem is in our own mind. Abolish the perception that there's a problem, and you may come to a solution.

- Make sure you're deciding from the right place.

- Don't be influenced so much by others; take in what you need but decide for yourself.

- You can't be certain, so the best you can do is decide as best you can.

- Those that think they know, know not.

We usually base our decisions on the following:

- Reason - based on principle, not personal preference.

- Love - for others, for the work at hand.

- Virtue - conformity to a standard of right.

- Duty - from obligation or responsibility.

- Fear - avoidance or insecurity.

Do you know why you make the decisions you make? Is there one characteristic on the list above that guides you all the time?

My experience in the working world feels like 90% of the decisions made are based on Duty or Fear. *I have to do this because that's the way it's done,* or *I have to do this because I will beat that guy to the punch*, or *if we don't do this, even though I know it's not right, it will piss off the boss.*

Do you believe we could use more Reason at work? Reason dictates that we decide based on the information at hand, in the moment, the power to infer what's best in a situation not from your ego, but what is the good of all. Reason also encourages us to make decisions from a fresh perspective, all the time, every time.

The Same Old Same Old Spells T.R.O.U.B.L.E

You've seen that report a gazillion times, you know what it's going to say and what you have to do because of it. But what if this time, you took the information as if you had never seen it before and started asking questions. Is there another way to look at it? What else is missing? What could make it better? Do you even need it anymore? Are you driving your employees nuts, forcing them to generate this report, when in actuality, it means nothing, and it serves nothing?

Decisions, Decisions!

So based on what our philosopher friends offered, here are a few things you can practice at work to cultivate more deliberation and make your decision making stronger:

Deliberation Practice

Note the basis of your decisions. Are you making decisions from a Reasoned place or a Fear-based place? Every day for a week, at the end of the day, write down one or two decisions you made (big ones, not that you decided on a latte instead of your usual Americano). Think about the basis for decisions, which ones apply? If you know why you're making your decisions, and you realize you're not using enough Reason, you can begin the steps of being driven by Reason instead of being driven by fear or insecurity.

Cultivate fairness, kindness, and truth. Every day, pick one. Today you're going to be fair. Decide what that means. Are you not going to take someone's word over another's? Are you going to weigh a decision more carefully? Or let's say, you decide to practice kindness. Is there an employee that's been struggling with whom you haven't had time to check in? Or perhaps you're upset at them: what if you were nice to them, and let it go for a day? Or you choose truth. Let's say you're contemplating a restructuring: are you clear on why you're doing it, or are you doing it because you think that's the solution? What's true of the situation that warrants a restructuring?

Say "I don't know," even if you think you know. Socrates said "I know that I know not, and that makes me a wise man." This is one of my absolute favorite practices. Spend a day not knowing. Sit from the position of maybe you don't know everything. If someone asks you for an opinion, genuinely say, "I don't know," and then take the time to make sure you investigate or feel you can provide a Reasoned answer. Being in "I don't know" mode also releases your mind to discover new solutions and ideas. If you constantly believe you know everything (which is impossible, remember what Voltaire said), then there's no impetus for your mind to be creative or continue to look for new information.

I "Need It Now" Version

Let's say you're in a pressure cooker situation - you have until the end of the day to make a decision on something big. You need to tap into that innate wisdom STAT. Here's what you do: whatever the decision, **go with the one that has the best outcome for all involved.** If that means it's what's best for your customers, so be it. If it means it's what's best for the team, then that's the right thing to do. Forget about yourself, or your panicky peanut gallery, for a moment, and think about the impact for all involved. **That's the right call, every time.**

Deliberate About Deliberation

Here's what happened when people were deliberate about deliberating.

> "I think I found myself trying really hard to pause and not just jump into a reaction, which I think helped me in a lot of situations where I would by nature just jump right in and say, 'Let me tell you what I think,' versus trying to literally pause and not say anything. I now think about it for a minute, before I respond, and then I offer a thoughtful answer as opposed to a flippant response that would be more out of emotion than intelligence." - **Sales Consulting Firm CEO**

> "I was more deliberate in my vision this past week. I've been really focusing on listening, as well as practicing the fairness, kindness idea, and trying to determine what I say and how I make a decision and how it might impact others. I was thinking through that process a little bit more carefully, especially in terms of considering the impact before I make the decision. I caught myself before saying something or deciding on something. I also tried to put myself in the other person's shoes. The principles were definitely at work." - **Head of Employee Engagement, State Government**

"This is a practice that I'm trying to bring into more of my work because the speed of everyday life is sort of conditioned. You react rather than deliberate. I think there's also a lot of benefit from being able to say, 'I don't have an answer right now because I need to think about this.' Or even say, 'I don't know, but give me a chance to think about it, and then let's discuss it.' I have found this exercise more often leads me to the right answer than just giving an answer in the middle of the moment." - **Chief Strategy Officer, Advertising Firm**

Action: When the Stop Gets Going

"True power is restraint." - Warren Buffet

All Booked Up with Nowhere to Go

Your calendar looks like a game of Tetris. It's the third day in a row you're eating lunch at 3 p.m., or maybe, 8 p.m. What's up with that person who talks a good game but doesn't really *do* anything? Or the one who's constantly going off and doing random stuff, but no one has any idea what they're doing or why they're even doing it? Or someone whose get up and go has got up and went? Perhaps, even, you yourself have been in idea mode for what seems like eternity. Or maybe even worse, you haven't had an idea in such a long time that work feels rote, and you think people are starting to notice (remember to watch for those pesky thoughts!).

Action and inaction quandaries come from the same source so now we're going to approach doing things from a wise place. If you've grounded yourself in reality, if you've really sorted out your thoughts and you know where they're coming from, and you've actually taken a minute to decide things, then now:

It's time to act.

What I love about the principle of action is that it reveals that philosophy isn't this thing that just sits by itself in an ivory tower, and that the only thing philosophers do is sit around and think wise thoughts all the time.

Believe it or not, philosophy really, truly **teaches us how to act.**

It helps us and our ability to negotiate and operate in the real world, and it remains a protocol for engaging with the world.

This is where you plug in. This is where you actually do the right thing. So, the question remains: how do you do the right thing? Philosophy not only tries to get us to see and identify the right thing to do, but it can also help us strike a balance around doing it.

Balance, in this principle, reigns supreme. Action's natural law proposes that you:

- Start from non-action.
- Then, from non-action,
- You have an impulse.
- Then you act.
- Then, you return to non-action.

This sequence represents the five states of action. Here's where it gets especially interesting:

Non-action ranks just as important as action.

We're going to explore this a little bit further, as non-action seems almost heretical.

In today's working world, constant action is emphasized, and it's reinforced over and over again, but that's not sustainable.

Somehow, we have put value on being hyper-busy as a marker of success. "Hustle porn," they call it. You learn that some CEO says they wake up at 3 a.m., and the thought that immediately crosses your mind is "Should I do that?" We all know about the "entrepreneurial grind," and we all know consultants and executives who regularly work seven days a week.

How do I know that this doesn't work? Oh, maybe because people are suffering burnout in record numbers, and some pick up drinking or rely on more serious substances to cope with this addiction to such a frenetic pace of action.

I took a look at the professions that had the highest rate of alcoholism and ... it was almost every profession.

Not kidding: According to Alcohol.org, lawyers, healthcare professionals, mining, construction, hospitality and food services, arts and entertainment, management, real estate, finance and insurance, educational services all have higher than the national average rate of alcohol consumption.

That's practically, well, everyone. Except philosophers. (Wink, wink. Nudge, nudge.)

All kidding aside though, job and money troubles rank as the top reason for suicides according to the Center for Disease Control.

So this begs the question: if constant action is so great, why are people so out of control?

In my experience, the answer to this and other questions is there's not enough stopping. Most people don't stop, and most people don't really ever get to feel the experience of well and truly being done with something, truly being closed with it, and then pausing before moving on to the next thing.

The most prominent example of this is our preoccupation with multitasking. So many experts and consultants advise us not to multitask, but so many of us pay only lip service to this. When you multitask, you're never really truly done with anything. You might think you are, but that's just your hyped-up mind talking, saying something along the lines of "I'm multitasking, and we're multitasking so we must be really doing something *awesome*."

In actuality, you're not moving forward one bit, and you're not really giving yourself the chance to finish anything that you started.

And yes, it's truly better to be done than to be perfect. The key here is to know when you're truly well and done, or if you're just rushing something off to cross something off on your to-do list. It's to know when it feels right, or if it feels like you're leaning into perfectionism.

Building in some white space right along with the activity, hitting the pause button in between the fast-forward key, is just as important as being on the move, in the groove, and doing things.

To Act or Not to Act, that is the Question

Action and Non-Action Serve Each Other

To delve more fully into the philosophy of action, we're travelling to China and India to see what philosophers there can say about this important principle, and specifically, we're going to listen to the words of Lao Tzu, Sri Shantananda Saraswati, and Vivekananda.

Lao Tzu was about not acting and being in that place. Sri Shantananda Saraswati was all about what is the measure and the process of action. Vivekananda taught us to be wary of the desire for outcomes.

Let's review the stages of action. The measures of action come along in four stages: when we are not acting, we are at rest, when we experience another impulse, thought or inclination, and then when we move into action again. When that cycle is completed, we rest, and it cycles again.

The Measures of Action

rest → impulse→action → rest

(this is real flow)

This is the process of *real* flow.

Let me restate this: this is the process of *real* flow.

There's this idea of flow, which is: you're in the activity, you are the activity. It's such an elegant idea! What I'm saying is if we expand our view of what is the context, and what surrounds the activity, almost zooming out to the view of the entire day around that activity, there's actually a whole bigger plane of existence and way of being that contributes to the real flow.

Action, in its entirety is actually: to be at rest, to have a proper impulse to act, and then to rest, again.

How does proper flow of action impact decision making? To best understand this, is to know in what balance those measures are specifically when they're out of whack. To more fully understand this, let's first consider and contemplate what Lao Tzu, Sri Shantananda Saraswati, and Vivekananda directly say about Action.

Non-Action and Action and How They Serve Each Other

"Empty yourself of everything.

Let the mind rest at peace.

The ten thousand things rise and fall
while the Self watches their return.

They grow and flourish and then
return to the source.

Returning to the source is stillness,
which is the way of nature.

The way of nature is unchanging.

Knowing constancy is insight.

Not knowing constancy leads to
disaster.

Knowing constancy, the mind is
open.

With an open mind, you will be
openhearted.

Being openhearted, you will act
royally.

Being royal, you will attain the
divine."

Lao Tzu

"The sage acts without pressure from within or without." - Sri Shantananda Saraswati

"A disciplined mind is very peaceful.

Fullness of discipline ultimately means being faithful in oneself.

Discipline simply means moving freely." - Sri Shantananda Saraswati

"One of the greatest lessons I have learnt in my life is to pay as much attention to the means of work as to its end. I have always been learning great lessons from that one principle, and it appears to me that all the secret of success is there; to pay as much attention to the means as to the end.

Our great defect in life is that we are so much drawn to the ideal, the goal is so much more enchanting, so much more alluring, so much bigger in our mental horizon, that we lose sight of the details altogether.

But whenever failure comes, if we analyze it critically, in ninety-nine percent of cases we shall find that it was because we did not pay attention to the means. Proper attention to the finishing, strengthening, of the means is what we need. With the means all right, the end must come."
- Vivekananda from "Work and Its Secret"

True Action in Action

What the philosophers are saying is:

- Action should not be concerned about the outcome.
- Decisions should be made from a place of stillness.
- We learn from and merit success in the process.
- Do not be pressured to act.

As I mentioned before, it's easier to understand how to balance the measures of action when we relate to how they are when they are out of balance.

Too much rest -> disengaged, lethargic, staring at your screen, heaviness, having a hard time "getting going" or focusing.

Too much impulse -> constantly in idea mode, mind racing, feeling over energetic of mind, mania, scattered focus, and restlessness.

Too much action -> busyness, constantly moving from one thing to the next without stopping, operating on autopilot, you feel "You're just a machine, cranking it out," or the day usually ends with feeling like "What the heck just happened?"

I believe many people live in the "too much" state of being at work.

Sri Shantananda Saraswati provides guidance on what it feels like and looks like to act well or not.

"In the course of good actions, thoughts, and feelings, the body responds naturally, harmoniously, and mind supports them without any worry, distraction, or hesitation. Reason supports them with authority, the heart responds openly, the whole being supports them. There is nothing to hide, nothing painful, it is good for the one who does it and for all who are related to it; happiness prevails. All is agreeable within and without. When the action is good, then the outcome is auspicious.

"A bad action, thought, or feeling is that which is concealed, done in the dark; the body is not free, mind does not freely support, reason opposes, heart cries, fear prevails, and displeasure is felt within and without. It harms the individual and others. It is bound, limited, and heavy; only habit supports such actions. The outcome of such actions, thoughts, and feelings is inauspicious." - Sri Shantananda Saraswati

How to Act with Tact

So if we understand how action and non-action serve each other, then we can say the right thing to do, the right way to act stems from those two states coming together in balance.

You can't have the proper use of one without the proper use of the other. It's this Yin and Yang, a perfect balance between action and non-action. You will know, or you will get the answer, or you will be able to act properly, if both of these things are in balance with each other. When they are out of balance, we do things not in a thoughtful way, or we do them absentmindedly, or we do them in overdrive.

Action serves a purpose, but inaction also serves a purpose, and sometimes it's better to not act than to act.

If you do this, then you're going to better execute your thinking, vision, and ideas.

Action Practice

Since there's a chance you may be in a place of too much rest, too much impulse, or too much action, here are some ways to bring these states into further balance:

Too much rest - > Be of service: help someone, help an employee, help a colleague, see where maybe your attention can be outside of you. This is a really incredibly powerful practice because being of service can get you out of your own lethargy very quickly. It also feels very fulfilling. If you can't think of what to do for yourself, if you can't think of your own work, or how to tackle your own work, just think of someone who you know who might need help. From that point on, you're going to get a good impulse, and then all of a sudden you're off to the races.

Too much impulse -> Notice your environment: when there's that constant ideation, that kind of mania-like existence completely in your head, practice awareness. What that means is to immediately recognize the environment that you're in, bring yourself into what is happening in the moment, at that moment. If you continue to do that, then the period of time that you're in too much impulse decreases, and the next step, which is action, is much more likely to be achieved.

Too much action -> Stop and ask: what am I valuing now? Let's say you are in that hamster wheel, running around autopilot, living in the state of extreme busyness. When you catch yourself doing that, immediately ask yourself this very important question:

What am I valuing now? Are you valuing hard work, or are you giving yourself a badge of honor for being busy? Are you valuing what people think of you or your actual contributions? Typically, when we live in a state of too much action, it's because we're living in fear of repercussions, we're working in martyr mode, or we're stuck in a state of overexcitement. This practice forces you to understand the underlying reasons for your overactivity so you can be aware of them and address them, and thus, bring things down a bit.

I "Need It Now" Version

You have to do something right now. There's no time to dilly-dally, and you've taken in all the information you can on the matter. **Before you do anything,** *pause.* Like the financial advisor you encountered earlier in this book, follow his advice, and wait. Take a minute, you have that amount of time, and pause before you proceed. Act from that split-second of stillness and let your mind orient around what you are about to do. Then do it.

Caught in the Act!

These very wise executives practiced non-action and action for a week. This is what they said about their experience:

"I was feeling bitter about something that didn't go my way. I felt myself sulking. I was in a "why me" kind of a state. But I had to get back to work, there were like a million things going on, and I just couldn't bring myself to work on anything. I was talking to one of my employees, and they had a question about something. A simple thing they didn't know how to do. Here is where I remembered the"being of service" idea. I decided to really dive in to answer their question, went to their desk, sat, and listened to what the issue was, and then walked them through what to do. I felt less cranky after that, and I think they appreciated the extra attention. Then, I had a bit more energy and was able to move onto something else." - **Director of Marketing, Broadcast Network**

"I didn't realize how bad things were until I stopped. I couldn't shut my brain off at all. You know that cartoon of the octopus that's doing a bunch of things at the same time? That guy was in my head. I saw how neglectful I had been to my work. No wonder I felt stuck. I wasn't moving forward with anything because I wasn't taking the time to even know what I was supposed to be moving forward about! I wasn't making big decisions, just a

bunch of small little ones that barely moved the needle or my career."-**Manager, Health Care Services Start-Up**

"It was close to eight o'clock at night, and a partner had just decided to completely restructure an entire presentation I had been working on. It made the presentation better, but it added several hours to an already tight deadline. I was exhausted, fried, overwhelmed by the changes, and I could feel myself shutting down. I thought to myself, "What am I valuing now?" At first, I was like, why am I here, what am I doing...I'm going to be here until midnight! However, I knew I was in "thoughts" and focused on what was of value here at this moment. I asked myself again: "What am I valuing now?" and the answer that came back was: "the idea." The idea we were presenting would help our client help other people. Once I came to the realization that I needed to value the idea, it wasn't about the partner's last-minute changes anymore. It wasn't about my fading energy. It was about something bigger, and it was ultimately about helping people. With that, I allowed myself a quick pause to rest my mind a bit, and I had a renewed sense of energy." - **Marketing Strategist, Publishing Company**

Final Thoughts

Hopefully, you've learned how philosophy and wisdom can be a great tool to use at work.

Work should not be mechanical and habitual. It should be fresh and attentive.

Remember my CMO client who was in the pit of despair? After applying the ideas I gave him, the ideas you've read about here in this book, he now has a whole new program and body of work he's using with his clients, and he's consistently achieving excellent results. "I feel more energized about work now," he says. "I feel like I'm making a real contribution, and I'm now acting from a foundational place. It's not like my life or my work is perfect, but I don't need perfection in order to be productive and calm."

Because he's decluttered his overthinking, he's now clear about what he wants to do, what he needs to do, and he can now do the work to the best of his abilities. "My meetings have more purpose, and my conversations are more direct and clearer," he says. "When those 'out-of-sync' feelings come up, I actually embrace them now as a chance to dig a little deeper on my thoughts and decisions." In short, he's content, and he's optimistic about both his future and his work.

Wisdom needs to be cultivated in order to work. It may not always be easy to remember, and it does require practice, but as you have seen in the examples in this book, it is possible and extremely beneficial for you and for those you work with.

From being calmer to seeing solutions to nagging problems (and people), wisdom can help you have a better understanding and relationship with yourself and your work. If you can glimpse even for a minute what my clients and I have experienced, you might see a positive outcome to something that's really important to you at work.

So, try these practices, work through these ideas, and see what happens!

"To lead with wisdom is to create an organization infused with wisdom which puts that wisdom out in the world through its work, and shows its employees, customers, and eventually society the way of wisdom. This is the work we want to do and the world we want to live in." - Cristina DiGiacomo

Lead wisely!

Acknowledgements

For those who help connect me to my existence - Mustapha Louafi, my friends and my family.

For those who help me attain knowledge - all the tutors and students at The School of Practical Philosophy. My main man, Socrates. All philosophers everywhere, whoever and whenever you are. The New School. All the bosses and co-workers I ever had.

For those who helped bring my ideas into reality - Jeff Loehr - marketing, Heather Schooler - coach, Ben Gioia - book-writing consultant, Jeanette Hurt - editor, and Belinda Goodrich - publisher.

A special thanks to Jeffrey Hayzlett for your kind words and all the people of the C-Suite Network for your support.

About Cristina DiGiacomo

Cristina DiGiacomo is an Industrial Philosopher who teaches executives who care about engagement how to cultivate the ultimate soft skill - wisdom. She combines 20 years of experience in the working world in  strategy and management roles at companies such as Citigroup, AMC Networks, The New York Times, and R/GA.

She has a Master of Science in Organizational Change Management, and she has been a student at The School of Practical Philosophy since 2011. She has presented to faculty her work on Industrial Philosophy at The New School and is writing a paper on "The Just Organization," connecting principles of philosophy around justice and how to develop an equitable and just organizational culture for the American Management Association.

She has been a guest on the television program *CEO Chat* and is on Jeffrey Hayzlett's C-Suite Network's *Thought Council*. She is currently the Vice President of the Organization Development Network of New York and is a member of the Society for Human Resources Management and the Association for Talent Development. She lives in Forest Hills, Queens.

Made in the USA
San Bernardino, CA
21 April 2020